THE
Old Photographs
SERIES

ELLESMERE PORT

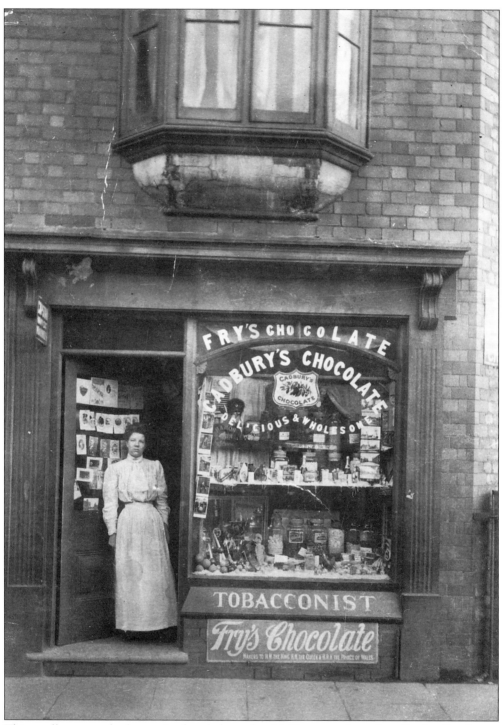

This small sweet and tobacconist shop belonged to M. Foster, and stood on Station Road next to the Post Office and opposite Queen Street. Like other tobacconists of that period, they sold local postcards with their own name on and sometimes exclusive to that shop. This is one of them.

THE
Old Photographs
SERIES

ELLESMERE PORT

Compiled by
Pat O'Brien

**ALAN
SUTTON**

BATH • AUGUSTA • RENNES

First published 1994
Copyright © Pat O'Brien, 1994

Alan Sutton Limited
12 Riverside Court
Bath BA2 3DZ

ISBN 0 7524 0023 1

Typesetting and origination
by Alan Sutton Limited
Printed in Great Britain

A scene in Chester Road, Whitby in the early years of the century.

Contents

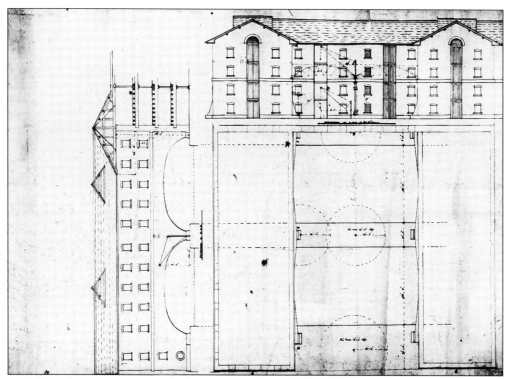

Ground and elevation plans for Teleford's Warehouse of 1840.

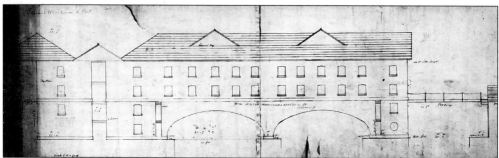

The Riveracre Road seen here in the 1930s was once the main road from Whitby village to Birkenhead.

Introduction

In two previous books on Ellesmere Port I have used a more formal approach to the telling of the town's history but in this volume I have presented a more visual story. Using old photographs I describe the growth of the Port and also something of the lives of its people over the last hundred years. The core of this collection of images is postcards of the period but the book also uses other photographs taken by both amateurs and professionals.

F. Walker, who ran a post-office and chemists shop in Little Sutton was also a photographer and recorded the local scene with a series of postcards which he sold from his shop. He did not apparently have a studio and I have never come across any portraits that he made but I have used several of his street scenes from the period 1900 to 1920 in this book. His pictures are captioned in a distinctive and recognisable fashion. At about the same time a photographer called W. Hall from Widnes was also active in the area and some of his vibrant street and industrial scenes are featured in this book.

But important as these commercial pictures are it is the record of life that is preserved in family albums that brings social history to life. Photographs of schools, weddings, sporting life and other local events preserve for ever memories that would otherwise have faded and been lost for ever.

The villages around Ellesmere Port still retain some individuality and have origins that go back much further that the town itself. Hooton and Little and Great Sutton are all mentioned in the Domesday Book though spelt a little differently from today. Whitby also has early associations since the name is derived from a Norse word and was once, perhaps, a Viking settlement.

Ellesmere Port itself arose from Whitby Locks, the name by which the locks in the Canal Basin were originally known. The name gradually changed to the Port of Ellesmere and finally, by the early nineteenth century, to Ellesmere Port. The first housing grew up around the docks and the first main street was Dock Street. Station Road was gradually developed and as more shops were needed so some of these houses became retail premises. These changes are illustrated clearly in the pages of this book. Industry was attracted to the dockland areas because of the possibility of easy transport and access to raw materials from further afield. The growth of industry led to the growth of new housing to accommodate the influx of new workers and their families. Area and street names can often identify who the streets were built by (eg. Shropshire Row after the Canal Company) or where they came from (Wolverham after the Wolverhampton Corrugated Iron Company). Many of these early industries have now gone from this area or have declined because of changing demands. The rusted remains of some of them still remain to remind us of what was once here, like fossils of our industrial heritage.

Photographs create different memories for different people, some created by these pictures will be happy ones and some, though hopefully not too many, will be sad ones. To the younger Ellesmere Port residents these pictures will show a town that is only vaguely recognisable to them through remnants of old buildings that survive between the new and deserted factories that once buzzed with activity but are now silent or have found another use. This collection of old photographs covers all aspects of work and play for all kinds of people who have lived and worked here for a period of more than a hundred years. I hope you enjoy looking through them.

Pat O'Brien
Ellesmere Port
1994

One

The Canal Basin
and the Docks

A ship is berthed in the Tidal Lock on the left and it must be high tide in the estuary because the inner gates to the docks are open and the water on both sides is level. Opposite the lighthouse stands the Lower Pumping Station, this supplied hydraulic power to cranes on the North Wall, the Coal Tip, and the Clay Warehouses.

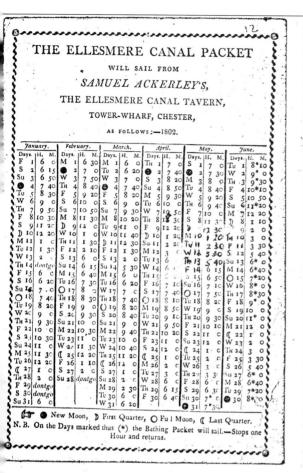

THE ELLESMERE CANAL PACKET

WILL SAIL FROM

SAMUEL ACKERLEY'S,

THE ELLESMERE CANAL TAVERN,

TOWER-WHARF, CHESTER,

AS FOLLOWS:—1802.

January.		February.		March.		April.		May.		June.	
Days.	H. M.	Days.	H. M.	Days.	H. M.	Days.	H. M.	Days.	H. M.	Days.	H. M.

(six-column monthly tide/sailing tables, January to June)

● New Moon, ☽ First Quarter, ○ Full Moon, ☾ Last Quarter.

N.B. On the Days marked thus (*) the Bathing Packet will sail.—Stops one Hour and returns.

July.		August.		September.		October.		November.		December.	
Days.	H. M.	Days.	H. M.	Days.	H. M.	Days.	H. M.	Days.	H. M.	Days.	H. M.

(six-column monthly tide/sailing tables, July to December)

Fare in the best Apartment, from Chester to Liverpool, 2s. 6d.; in the second Apartment, 1s. 6d.—Fare along the Canal and back, 2s. and 1s. 6d.

Parcels and Luggage are taken in at the Ellesmere Canal Tavern, Tower-wharf, where Information may be had respecting the Packet.

N.B. In the Passage from Chester to Liverpool, the Whole of the Fare is to be paid to the Captain of the Canal Packet, who will deliver a Ticket to each Passenger, which will free the Liverpool Packet; and in the Passage from Liverpool to Chester, the same must be done with the Captain of the Liverpool Packet, whose Ticket will free the Canal Packet.—The Proprietors will not be accountable for any Parcel above five Pounds Value, unless paid for as such; not for any Parcel or Luggage, unless duly entered—An elegant Packet for Bathers, at 1s. 6d. and 1s. each Person, during the Season.—On the Day not appointed for bathing, the said Boat may be hired by Parties of Pleasure the whole Day, for 1l. 10s. exclusive of any other Expence whatever.

Chester, Fletcher print.

A timetable for the Ellesmere Canal Packet which travelled between Chester and Ellesmere Port. The sailings were frequent and at Ellesmere Port people who had bought a ticket for Liverpool would change here to the Liverpool Packet. There were also special Bathing Packet boats, to the bathing huts and shooting butts among the dunes, all shown on a plan of the Canal Terminal of 1802.

A close up view of the Tidal Lock occupied by a coastal sailing ship. The warehouses were built in the 1860s for the Potteries traffic, holding crates of pottery and China Clay from Cornwall.

In the days before the Ship Canal was built, shipping was mainly under sail, as this view of the Main Dock area, probably in the 1860s, shows.

Here is a unique photograph showing two entrances into the port and docks. During the building of the Ship Canal it was decided to build a new entrance into the docks, and do away with the old one on the right of the lighthouse. After much deliberation it was decided to fill the new entrance in and retain the old one.

At the end of January 1890 the sea wall separating Ellesmere Port from the estuary was assuming gigantic proportions. This huge embankment was started from the centre nearly opposite the old dock entrance.

When the embankment was completed a railway was constructed on the top of it and the workmen no longer required on the Ellesmere Port section and who had lodgings there, would now travel by train to the Ince section.

During the building of the Ship Canal it was decided that the land either side of the lighthouse would be made into quays. In May 1892 the Pyrope was the first ship to use them.

It took three attempts to fill in the gap in the embankment opposite the docks, from the 11th to the 16th of July 1891.

The key in the foreground was an important instrument in the hydraulic network, directing pressure or shutting off leaking lines.

Entering the Ship Canal Ellesmere Port, in about 1900.

To the right of the tugboat is "Ivy House" where the S.U.R.C. Co. Agent lived. Its ivy-clad walls lived up to its name (Michael Day Collection).

The river lock was known as "Nicholas Lock" after its first lock gateman W. Nicholas. He and his brother came here from Frodsham when the docks were first made.

This is the swing bridge over the canal arm that went to the Flour Mills constructed in 1904. The children probably came from Primrose Hill, the name given to the area including Union and Back Union Streets and Shropshire Row.

On the little hill behind the stern end of the coastal steamer can be seen the Mersey Mission to Seamen Church known as the Bethell. Its first missioner was Mr John Howard whose family today still own his bible.

Since the 1850s coastal shipping brought cargoes of iron ore from the ports of Whitehaven and Ullverston to the Iron Raddle Wharf for use by the iron trades of the Black Country. From Ellesemere Port it was loaded into narrow boats and taken down the "Shroppie".

The end of Shropshire Row can be seen on the left. These houses were built in alternate pairs of two-storied and three-storied houses, the latter to cater for larger families. This view of 1908 shows that the Grain Elevator is busy.

Early in 1927 work started to extend the Ship Canal Docks from the Coal Tip to a considerable distance beyond Mount Manisty on the far side. Rail lines were linked to the existing ones, and new types of cranes installed.

This view shows the full extent of the docks before the extension of wharfs. In the distant background can be seen Mount Manisty built of spoil from the making of the canal and named after the engineer Mr Manisty.

The Pier Head was a popular place to wheel the pram and for elderly people to sit and view the passing events.

This shows the start of the excavation work to extend the new bunkering installations which could give ships a quicker turn around.

By deepening the water here and as far as Eastham to 28 feet, port charges at Liverpool could be avoided by shipping export goods to Ellesmere Port and loading them here onto bigger ships.

Because there is no longer a Tidal Lock there is no need by this time, for lock gates to control the level in the inner docks.

The uncrowded centre gives a good view of Telford's Warehouse in the centre of the picture and the Clay and Grain Warehouses on the left with their hydraulic cranes. At the Iron Ore Wharf on the right is a coaster unloading a cargo of iron ore.

On the 31st March 1970 a disasterous fire engulfed Telford's Warehouse. It was attended by ten fire appliances, and the smoke from the fire was seen many miles away.

Sadly, because of the total devastation, the buildings were later demolished. The width of the arches was such that it was believed that the centre part of the arches must have been held up by rods coming down from the roof. During demolition these were not found, but when the basin was emptied a matching bottom arch was found under the water and this provided the support.

Boarding up the approach to Telford's Warehouse from Grosvenor Wharf on the day after the fire. A meeting after the fire led to the eventual preservation of what was left and the establishment of the Boat Museum.

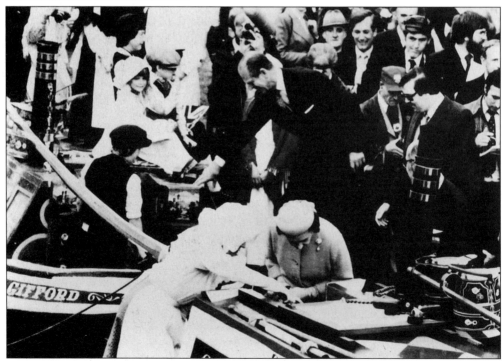

The Boat Museum was opened in 1976 after six years of hard work by school children and people from all walks of life. This photograph shows a Royal Visit from the Queen and Prince Philip in 1979. (Photograph by Colin Pitcher).

Two
Industry

An official dispatch card issued by King's Flour Mills to tell customers that their order had been forwarded to them and was on its way. This one is postmarked 29th July 1921.

Here is a distant view of the elevated rail sidings that led down to the coal wharf photographed in 1908. The main building is the flour mill with the grain elevator on its left.

A close up of the Coal Tip taken at the same time. It also shows the giant hydraulic lifts in the foreground that could elevate coal waggons and tip their loads onto the ships.

Another view of the Imperial Flour Mills on the left, with the uncompleted King's Mill on the right. Both mills were later to be extended bringing them closer together.

Imperial and King's Mills, seen here later, are now joined by a third mill on the extreme right, Frosts from Chester. In this view taken after 1910, the chimney stack of King's Mill is almost obscured by the new extensions.

The imperial Flour Mill was the first of the three flour mills to be built. It was completed in late 1905 and contained two complete milling plants, milling operations commencing soon as the first one was installed. With the canal arm at the rear and rail sidings at the front, finished

sacked goods to be distribued could pass to either side for transporting. The labour force was not large, in 1921 they were employing only 50 men.

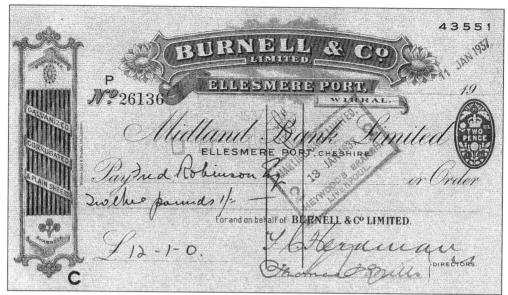

A company cheque for Burnell & Sons, the oldest of two metal working firms in Ellesmere Port. Burnells came here in 1879, twenty five years before the Wolverhampton Corrugated Iron Co. Ltd. Company cheques bearing company trade marks or symbols are becoming fashionable again today.

The Wolverhampton Corrugated Iron Co. Ltd. came here from the Midlands in 1904. They brought with them from Wolverhampton a large part of their workforce to work at the new ironworks created here.

Sheet rolling mills of the Wolverhampton Congregated Iron Co. Each mill had a team, headed by a boss, the "Roller". In his team he had the heaver-over, the bar-dragger, the shearer, the doubler, the marker, the scaler, the breaker-down, the furnace man, and last, but not least, the scrapcutter.

Among the scrapcutter's duties was to go to the nearest pub in the afternoon and evenings for the beer for the thirsty millworkers. At night, as one lay in bed, the process of manufacturing corrugated iron sheets could be followed almost from beginning to end with the succession of characteristic sounds that rang out across the town.

Construction of a new canal basin within the Wolverhampton Corrugated Iron Works. Planks were inserted in the canal banks to form a dam while the work was carried out. The canal bridge is at the end of Cromwell Road.

This is the completed canal basin seen in construction above. There are two kinds of boats here, the narrow boats for Midland destinations, and the larger barges used to deliver to Chester, or transhipment at the ports of Birkenhead and Liverpool.

The Mersey Soap Works was one of the earliest industries at Ellesmere Port, founded in the 1860s by two brothers, Edward and Charles Davis. Workmen were employed by the soapery to hawk their products around the houses at 3d a bar. Eventually because of lack of sales the brothers split up and the works closed down in about 1875.

The man in the centre is William Clark whose father, also called William, moved to the town from Birkenhead and lived in Porters Row. William Junior is seen here with his colleagues and equipment of the Ellesmere Port Window Cleaning Co. For years he and his company were well known around the town. They are seen here in Station Road, in front of the Ellesmere Dairy, between 1914-18.

This was the Whitby Brickworks later called Pooltown Brickworks Ltd. This factory was at the end of a lane leading off Pooltown Road and the brick ovens extended beyond the sandpit in Capenhurst Lane. Local people called it "Bricky Ned's". The lane is now Loxdale Drive.

This group of building workers were probably building houses for workers of one of the industrial firms. This postcard was sent from Ashfield Road in 1912. The council did not build any houses until after 1919.

H.M. Ordnance Factory, Ellesmere Port. In October 1915 wartime demands made necessary increased production of phenol to make picric acid for explosives manufacture. A site was chosen at Ellesmere Port and five acres of land were rented from the Ship Canal Portland Cement Co. Ltd. By mid-February 1917 the construction of the factory was complete and the plant nearly ready to produce phenol. Because of the poor efficiency of the conversion process to picric, the factory was closed on the 26th February 1918. Picric had lost its importance in the manufacture of explosives and was soon replaced by amatol.

After closure the picric acid factory was converted for use as a Poison Gas Works. Here is the workforce at the Factory in 1918. The gentleman on the extreme right in the fourth row was Mr E.W. Capuano, an Australian engineer who worked at the factory in Ellesmere Port from 1917 to 1919. In letters home he described the conversion of the explosives factory into the Poison Gas works which was to be reconstructed by October 1918. It was completed and the gas ready for testing on schedule. On Sunday 3rd November there was an escape of gas and a high wind carried it to a village four miles away. It is not known whether there were any casualties but the incident stopped the church services! Fortunately, with the war ending, the gas was never used and the plant was shut down in February 1919.

The oil docks on the opposite side were once an island containing the site of the ancient monastic abbey of Stanlaw. When the Ship Canal was built the river Gowy that surrounded it was diverted underneath to flow through pipes into the estuary.

A group of riggers erecting installations at the Shell Mex Refinery in the 1930s. A local man, Mr Harry Lardner, is the fourth from the left at the top with an open-necked shirt.

1908 saw the construction of a dyeworks for the manufacture of synthetic indigo. When the first World War broke out the German owners had all the scientific and working records destroyed. Later it was taken over by the British firms continuing the production of indigo.

The construction of Bowaters Paper Mills began on a 55-acre site in 1929 and the mills came into production in 1931. They were later expanded in 1932. Houses on the Overpool Estate were reserved for those working at the paper mill.

An early company to locate specifically on the Ship Canal was the Manchester Ship Canal
Pontoons and Dry Docks Co. Ltd. This pontoon floating dock was capable of lifting vessels of
up to 2,500 tons.

Employees of McAlpines Depot in Ellesmere Port in 1932. Some names are known: front row,
left to right: J. Boyle, T. Wilkie, T. Barridan, G. Foden, W. Hollingworth, W. Davis and D.
Jones. Back row includes: H. Innes, M. Homer, E. Issacs, P. Oldham.

Lobitos Oil Refinery was built at Ellesmere Port in 1934. The company owned oil fields in Peru and a fleet of five tankers. Between 1942 and 1946 they refined oil from Nottinghamshire oil fields, and remained independant of overseas supplies.

The Lobitos Refinery Engineering Department in the 1950s.

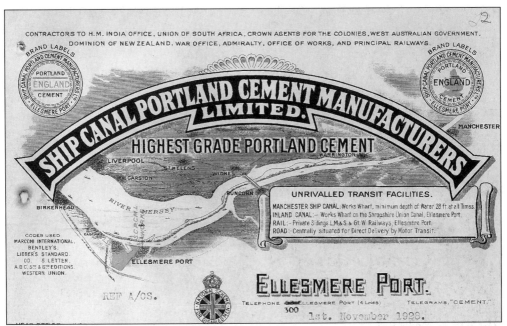

Up to about 1939 it was common practice for shops and firms to use the top of their billheads for publicity purposes. The pictorial content often showed the firms' location and, as here, gave transit facilities.

The Ship Canal Portland Cement Company factory was erected on the waterfront in 1911 and produced about 6,000 tons of high quality Portland Cement by the dry process per week. In 1921 the works ranked second as an employer in the town but price wars and keen competition forced its closure in 1932.

Employees of the Flour Mills gather outside by the railway sidings to celebrate their county regiment. The precise occasion is not known.

Vauxhalls started building their factory on part of the old Hooton airfield in 1961, and although operational by 1963, the first Viva did not roll off the assembly lines until the 1st June 1964. In this photograph the factory's first workers sign on for a day's work.

Three
Around Station Road

This view of Station Road was featured on another of Foster's series of postcards (see frontispiece). This scene is from the corner of King Street looking down Station Road c.1907.

In 1836 a Mr J. Brint bought some land on Primrose Hill and built himself a house which he named "Ivy House", and a tannery nearby. The house was later sold to the S.U. Canal Co. who retained it to be used by their agent. To local people it was known as "Bleak House" because of its stark appearance (Michael Day Collection).

Shropshire Row was one of a series of streets behind Ivy House. One of his inhabitants went out one night in about 1905 and disappeared. Although the dock was emptied and the canal dragged he was never found.

Stanley Road in about 1900. By the 1880s once isolated houses were being linked into streets, by rows of terraces, around the area of Dock Street. Small groups of villas were added to some streets such as, Brooklin Villas in Church Street (1887) and Hope Villas in Grosvenor Street (1886). Stanley Road began as Oak Avenue, in 1888.

Upper Mersey Street in the early years of the century. On the left-hand side is the Primitive Methodists' Central Hall, which was used as a school, as well as for religious purposes. It was built in 1872.

Dock Street became the first main street of the village of Ellesmere Port. To cater for the growing numbers of workers there were three public houses, the Bull's Head Inn, the Dock Hotel, and the Grosvenor Hotel (formerly known as The Grapes).

Dock Street in the 1950s. By this time the ground floor of many of the original houses had been converted into the street's first shops. Some of these remained with the houses' original families until this side of the street was demolished for the building of the motorway.

This is Dock Street in around 1910. The shop on the left is Ewart Stockton, Provision Dealer. Is that him standing next to the shop assistant in the apron? The boy with the basket could be the delivery boy but where is the bike? Notice the road sweeper with his brush and wheelbarrow and the narrow boat lady in the bonnet.

The Bull's Head Inn which stood at the corner of Dock Street and Station Road. Standing by the entrance is Mrs Catteral, wife of Joseph Catteral the landlord. Her son Tom, in later years, had an off-licence in Chester Road, Whitby.

Primitive Methodism in Ellesmere Port started off in the front room of a small cottage on Primrose Hill, belonging to John Stockton. When it became too small to accommodate all who wished to worship, a large room that was known as the Flatmen's Room over Tomkinson's Bakehouse was rented. Meetings were also held on Primrose Hill around the pump, the speaker occupying a cart brought there for purpose. This church was built in Queen Street in 1900.

48

The junction of Queen Street and Station Road in 1906. The shops are Marstons Cycle Shop and F.H.Butler, Fruiter & Grocer. There are notice boards on the far corner advertising a butcher's and an auctioneers, A. Jones & Co.

This is the bottom end of Station Road showing Foster's Post Office and W. H. Wilson's Public Saw Mills.

This Parish Church was the second to be built. The first church was built in 1846, but by 1868 was already too small, and work began on this one, closer to Station Road. This church was consecrated by Bishop Jacobson on the 16th May 1871.

An armistice service at the Parish Church War Memorial about 1928. In 1978 a new memorial to those killed in the Second World War was erected between the Civic Hall and the Library.

THE VICARAGE, ELLESMERE PORT. NO. 2112.

The Vicarage was described in 1906 as having a net yearly value of £320 with three acres of glebe and a residence, in the gift of the bishop of Chester, and held since 1903 by the Revd Oliver Edmund Rice.

The railings at the left are on the corner with King Street. Notice the path on the Vicarage side has not yet been paved.

Station Road in the early years of the century. Using the gas lamp in the middle as a reference you can compare this scene with the next picture to see the changes. The small shop in the background on the right stood on the corner of a future Carnegie Street.

Here we see the magnificent Old Post Office building at the corner of Carnegie Street. Notice the lamp post is now without a lamp! On the left, one house has been converted into a shop, J. Baker & Sons, Boot Dealers.

The Free Library was built at the corner of a new street by the Carnegie Trust in 1910. The new street was named Carnegie Street.

On the roof is a Victorian ventilation system. The wind rotated fan blades which created a draught inside, drawing all the bad air out and replacing it with fresh.

Parrs Bank stands at the corner of Westminister Road looking down Station Road to the corner of King Street. The only house that remains is number 108, two doors away from the corner. It still retains its bow windows.

Station Road from the corner of Cook Street. Bill posters can be seen on the gable end of the Cheshire Furnishing Stores in the background. The Post Office Building was later to be constructed on this site.

The wall on the left was a safeguard to a slope leading down to the cattle arch under the railway line. There was a lamp at the top of the slope to light the way down when it was dark.

This is the only view known that shows the Cattle Arch in its entirety and in association with the level crossing gates.

This is Station Road in 1930. In the trade directory of 1934 are listed the following shops: Manchester Stores, Drapers, at numbers 40 to 50; Pegrams, Grocers, number 52; the Maypole, at the number 54; F. H. Butler, Motor Haulage Contractor, at number 64.

This is the area between Carnegie Street and King Street in 1933. Some houses have been converted into shops, the nearest one on the left is Rowland Hill.

Four
Transport

A tugboat entering the locks at Eastham and heading for Ellesmere Port with a line of dumb barges. The cargo was grain for the mills. Tug skippers and crews were usually Ellesmere Port men.

The canal arm behind the mills. The larger barge on the right, Chester, would have been used only betwen Birkenhead Docks, Ellesmere Port, and Chester. The narrow boats were used for cargoes into the Midlands, along the narrower canals.

Although there were some privately owned canal boats the bulk of the cargoes were carried by boats owned by the S.U.R. Canal Co. like the one in the foreground. They ceased trading in 1921.

When the S.U.R.C. Company ceased trading the effect at their depot was the loss of jobs for 48 porters and 18 flatmen. This is believed to be a protest meeting called at the time (Michael Day Collection).

This is one of a fleet of steamer boats owned by the Wolverhampton Corrugated Iron Company on its way back to the works after passing Powell's Bridge (Michael Day Collection).

Although the waggons in this picture of the docks in about 1905 are marked London North Western, the small locomotive is not a main line one. It probably belongs to the Manchester Ship Canal Company (MSC) travelling on the line that skirted the Iron Raddle Wharf.

This a rare photograph of dock workers, clay pipes and all, posing for a photograph in a spare moment in about 1900. For some of the subjects this would have been the only photograph ever taken of them.

This locomotive, "Hamburg" (No 31), belonged to the Manchester Ship Canal Co. The engine driver was Andrew Agnew and the engine is now preserved at the Keighley & Worth Valley Railway Company.

This locomotive "Barry" belonged to the Ship Canal Portland Cement Manufacturers Ltd. They also had another loco named "Stanlow". When the works closed down it was kept as a shunt loco on the main line.

This locomotive belonged to the Smelting Corporation whose works were on a 60 acre site close to the ship canal with rail links to the main line. This is a Well tank locomotive (No 4), and its crew posed for this picture at the M.S.C. Wharf at Stanlow Meadows. Built by E.

Burrows & Sons of St. Helens in 1898 the engine works No. 37 is preserved today on the North Yorkshire Moors Railway. The locomotive driver is believed to be Mr A. Jones (Senior) of Ellesmere Port.

This locomotive belonged to the M.S.C. Company (No. 14). With the introduction of diesel locomotives there was no longer any need for a fireman, so the crew was reduced to a shunter and driver. This locomotive was a Hudswell Clarke 204 h.p. diesel. The shunter was Chris McCann and the engine driver, Raymond Agnew, the last of the Agnew family. He is also the little boy on a co-op trip on the ship Canal to be seen later (see Sports and Leisure).

This early locomotive (No. 81) is believed to have belonged to the Ship Canal Portland Cement Co.

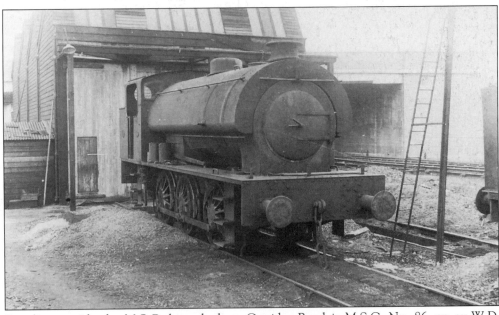

Standing outside the M.S.C. loco shed on Corridor Road is M.S.C. No. 86, an ex-W.D. Hudswell-Clarke.

This was the delivery dray for the London & North Western Railway Company which made deliveries on behalf of Ellesemere Port and Little Sutton Stations. A driver at one time was Mr Tommy Andrews (Michael Day Collection).

This oil-tanker was one of a fleet that belonged to British Viscoleum Fuels operating for Lobitos Refinery. It was a 3 ton, 6 cylinder, Commer. Its 3 tanks each held 300 gallons, emptied by a hand pump. It delivered to rural areas and the driver was Mr Tom Lardner.

H.M. Ordnance Factory, Ellesemere Port. This was the official transport for V.I.P.'s. visiting the Poison Gas works this time seen here outside the works in 1918.

Another picture, dated on the back 1919, of the official car transport for the factory seen here shortly before its closure.

This steam waggon was built by Sentinel (Shrewsbury) Ltd. for McAlpines in about -?- and was based at their great Stanney Plant Depot. Its unusual rear drive is thought to have been made for working in the Mersey Tunnel. (Michael Day Collection).

This is another waggon made by Sentinel, this time a steam waggon for general delivery purposes. (Michael Day Collection).

1914 TIME TABLE, CHESTER-ELLESMERE PORT. *Now a 15 minutes service.*

The first bus service between Ellesemere Port and Chester began in January 1911. It was started by Mr E. Crossland-Taylor using an Albion charabanc with hard tyres. This is a copy of an early timetable.

In 1913 Crosville extended their bus service betwen Ellesemere Port to include Birkenhead Tram Depot at New Ferry.

In 1919 a local man, Mr J.M. Hudson, started to run a bus service between Ellesemere Port and Chester. The vehicle was an ex-army ambulance adapted to seat 14 people. The bus operated until January 1922 (Michael Day Collection).

This Daimler charabanc belonged to Crosville Motors Ltd. and operated out of Chester just after the First World War. The background is Lower Mersey Street and the Imperial Flour Mills.

A steam engine belonging to timber merchant W.H. Wilson who started up here in the 1880s. Timber floats brought wood up to the east side of the dock, which was built almost level with the water and the cargo was discharged end on.

An early steamer of the Imperial Flour Mills c.1910. On the left is Edward Hamer with his brother William. The driver was Bob Price.

The arrival of the Helsby-bound train in 1908. Besides the Station Master, Mr H.H. Brice on the right, there are four porters in attendance. Notice the bill poster man with his bucket of paste and brush in the centre of the picture.

It is now 1910 and once again there is an assortment of passengers awaiting the Helsby train. Most of them appear to be students.

The Marquis of Westminster, who owned this land, would not sell it unless the railway would build a station here. From 1863 to 1870 the station was called Whitby Locks.

There were four signal boxes in the vicinity, this one was No.3 and had a wheel to operate the crossing gates. No.2 dealt with the sidings to the docks, and No.1 dealt with the main line. No.4, opposite Octel, is the only one now left.

This is the local road gang of the Cheshire County Council repairing the road in the 1930s. A local man, Fred Lardner, is standing second from the left. Notice the horse-drawn tar boiler.

A horse drawn refuse waggon. This team toured the cobblestoned lanes, between and around the backs of the houses. This is the lane that runs parallel to Princess Road and the railway line.

Five

Around Whitby Road

Whitby Road between 1930-31. The boardings on the right run from the last house in Stanlow Cottages to "Daddy Harts" at the corner of Princess Road. Some time after this Stanways Garage was built here and in 1932 a row of four shops called Broadway, were built on the land on the right.

One of the Foster Series of Postcards (No.294) sent on the 12th July 1907. The trees on the left stand where the corner of Victoria Road now is.

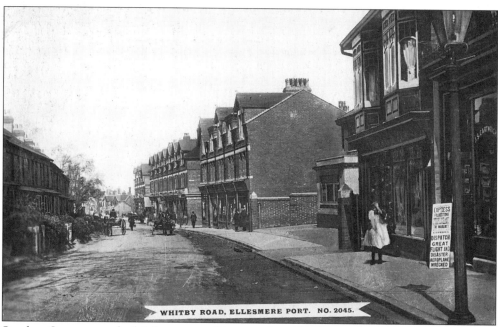

Stanlow Cottages on the left have now all been replaced by shops. This postcard is postmarked 1917.

This is the Stinton family outside their home in Stanlow Cottages before the First World War. They are, Dolly and Alf in front, with Jinny, Bill, and Arthur at the back. Arthur is now 90 years old.

Whitby Road in 1913. On the left is S.Jenkins, tobacconist and the Queens Cinema. Centre left is R.Baines & Sons, drapery stores, which had a pawnshop at the rear.

Whitby Road at the corner of Cromwell Road. On the corner was the Louvre and then shops were as follows; E. Preston and, next to him, Percy Crane, tobacconist and stationer (and publisher of this card). The postcard is postmarked 29th July 1926.

Men of the Cheshire Regiment form a guard of honour at the unveiling of a First World War memorial plaque outside Jones Ironworks in about 1924.

Afterwards the inspection. In morning dress is Berisford Jones and behind him, Mr Smiteman the caretaker of Cambridge Road School. The man in the bowler hat is Mr Kite and on his right is Mr Hamilton.

Whitby Street between 1932-33. On the right "Broadway" has been built. Most shops have their awnings down and can be identified from the names on them. The shop next to P. Cranes can be identified as Frisbys Shoe Stores.

On the left can be seen the cobbled entrance into Stanways Garage, and a pavement put down on this side alongside a fence, but no shops yet.

When Dudley Road was built in 1908 the houses were described as being in the same attractive style as some of the houses in Port Sunlight. This praise was justified, the architect was the same man, James Lomax Simpson.

The first Catholic Church in Ellesemere Port was the "Tin Church" built of corrugated sheets in 1909 in Enfield Road. Later a school was built alongside it .

A target map of Ellesemere Port taken by the Luftwaffe during the Second World War.

82

On the night of the 5th September 1940 the Luftwaffe dropped several bombs and land mines on Ellesemere Port and the surrounding area. Soldiers are seen here digging for unexploded bombs in the gardens of the William Stockton School.

On the back of the waggon is part of a land mine recovered near the school. On the left is a Corporal of the Royal Engineers in charge of recovering and removing the bombs seen here with a local Civil Defence worker.

These are the bombs found buried in the gardens and the girls playground. This school and the nearby Grange School were closed on the 6th and 7th September 1940 until the bombs were found.

Little Sutton Home Guard. There were units of the Home Guard in Ellesemere Port and Little Sutton, this is 'D' Company Cheshire (Little Sutton) Battalion with their C. O., S. V. Offley.

For a period after the Second World War the Auxiliary Fire Service and local works firemen, full and part time, would compete as teams in fire exercises in Whitby Park.

The Ellesmere Port & District Co-operative Society Ltd. was founded in November 1899. Their first shop was in Church Street and in 1914 they were also established at 25, Stanley Road. The picture shows the staff, standing in the doorway and the messenger boy in a white jacket.

There were two Maypole shops in Ellesemere Port, one in Station Road and the other in Whitby Road nearly opposite the Knot Hotel. This was taken outside the latter sometime in 1940 and shows two members of the staff, Peggy Whittaker (left) and Julia Rayner.

This group of shops was situated in Station Road between the Vicarage and Carnegie Street. From the left was The Midland Tailoring & Boot Co., the Port Drapery Co. and the Cheschire Furnishing stores. This postcard is dated 22nd June 1909.

Richard Jones was known to all as "Dicky" and his shop stood at the corner of King Street and Station Road. This view is from 1909. By 1914 he had moved to a site in Westminister Road.

Dysons stores was established at 37, Whitby Road in 1919. They later expanded to include No.39 and were here until 1937 before moving into Exeter Road. Third from left is Cyrill Mansell who later opened his own shop in Cambridge Road.

This is Perrys of Whitby Road. On the right is Mr perry and next to him are his two daughters. His wife is on the extreme left but the other lady has not been identified.

Originally known as Clegg Brothers, this shop in Whitby Road changed to W.G.Clegg. They had another shop in Queens Street. At the back, on the left is Fred Jones, standing with Walter Greaves Clegg. At the front from the left are Miss N.Clegg, Miss M.Clegg and Miss V.Nall.

Outside the family shop of W.Whittaker at 75, Oldfield Road. It traded between 1921 and 1942. In the family car are William and his wife Edith, and in the back are their daughter Peggy and son Allan. The picture was taken in 1926.

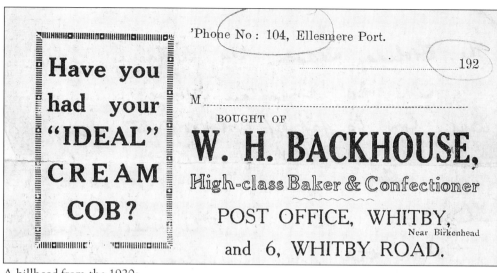

'Phone No : 104, Ellesmere Port.

192

M

BOUGHT OF

W. H. BACKHOUSE,

High-class Baker & Confectioner

POST OFFICE, WHITBY,

Near Birkenhead

and 6, WHITBY ROAD.

Have you had your "IDEAL" CREAM COB?

A billhead from the 1920s.

Mr W.H. Backhouse in 1911 set up a bakery and confectionery shop at the corner of Whitby and Vale Roads. Part of these premises were later converted into a Post Office. The advert for the "Ideal" cream cob over the Whitby shop, is repeated on his billhead above.

Some time after 1923 Mr W.H.Backhouse extended his business and opened a combined cafe and shop at number 6, Whitby Road, called the Ideal Bakery. Mr Backhouse's daughter, Lois, is the young lady in the tartan frock standing in the doorway.

Lloyds were wholesale and retail newsagents and tobacconists in Whitby Road for many years. To the left on the step is Alice Tolley and Mr Wheat, the shop manager, is in the background.

The first shop of G.H. Moss was situated at 63, Whitby Road. By 1934 the name over the door became G.H. Moss & Son. An additional shop for the firm came later in Chester Road, Whitby. Mr Moss, senior is in the foreground (Michael Day Collection).

The Manor Dairy in Whitby Road. Mrs Ithell, seen here, was the wife of the owner. This shop can also be seen in the bottom picture on page 110 (Michael Day Collection).

The open air market was always a popular feature of the town. Over the years it was held on many different sites, this particular one in the 1950s, was held inside York Road football ground.

The Methodist Church School in Merseyton Road in 1908. In the second row, second from the left, is Elizabeth Johnson, and next to her is her sister Georgina. Further along, numbers seven and eight, are (twins) Bertha, and Bessie Nuthall.

These boys and girls are celebrating May Day 1916. They were pupils of the Church School in Church Street. A pupil that has been identified is Mrs Phoebe Catteral (née Williams) in the second row, sixth from the right.

This is the Church Street, Church of England Rose Queen float on its way to the fete at Whitby Hall in 1922. On board are Maud Williams, Harriet Howard, Ida Harper, Gladys Griffiths, Elsie Penalberry and Winnie Foulkes.

This fancy dress party was held in 1929 at the church of England School in Arrowe Lane, also known as Miss Gerrard's School.

This charming group were photographed outside the Congregational Church that stood at the corner of Heathfield Road and Whitby Road. The nature of this event is not known.

A class at Cambridge Road School in the early 1920s. Standing in the background are the teacher Mr Roberts (left) and the headmaster Mr Munro. Some of the pupils were; W. Castree, T. Smeatham, T. Jobber and R. Hignett.

The staff of the Grange Boys Secondary School in 1959. Back row; left to right: A. Mort, T. Gormley, R. Shaw, L. Smith, G.T. Williams, J. Thomas, R. Stampe, W. Boyle, C. Jones. Front row incldes, but not necessarily in this order: R. Lewis, F. Wilkins, K. Young, W.D. Moorhouse, G. Evans, G. Davies, K. Faulkner, E. Gutteridge (Headmaster), G. Ford (Deputy Head), Mrs Jones (Sec).

A woodwork class in the Grange Evening Institute in 1956. Two keen ladies joined the men's class. One was a sister in the Cottage Hospital. The class instructor was Teg Williams.

This is the 1st Ellesemere Port Girl Guides photographed in the 1920s. In the centre of the back row is the captain, Miss Molly Wilding. In the background can be seen the Third Landing up the Ship Canal.

Ellesmere Port Catholic Boys Scouts in 1927. In the centre are Canon Curran and Scout Master J. Monagan. Others include: H.B. Worthington, T. Wilkie, F.S. Treet, T. Boyson, D. Heath, W. Bradley, H. Lalley, R. Bellingham, G. Rimmer, G. Dean, J. Lynch, J. Doyle, J. McNay, T. McCone, T. Gorman, J. Kelly, A. Birch and J. Beresford.

This group from the Independent Order of Oddfellows belonged to the Ellesmere Port Lodge. There was also a lodge in Little Sutton which staged annual walks around the village.

The Catterals and the Percivals were two well-known local families. On the left (seated) is Mr C.Percival with his wife behind him, and his soldier son Ellis. On the right is Mr J.Catteral (seated) with his wife, and on the extreme left, his son Thomas and on the right, his other son, Joseph M.

The wedding day of Mr V.Sallis and Miss Foxhall. Mr Sallis was a cobbler and worked from a small hut on the curve of Chester Road leading down to Vale Road (See p. 113).

The Eggingtons' governess trap with farmer Williams' pony "Dolly". Miss Williams is holding the reins and in the trap are Miss Jones, Miss Backhouse amd Miss Beech.

Enfield Road dressed in flags and buntings for the Coronation of George VI and Queen Elizabeth, May 1936.

Grange Road Coronation festivities in 1936. Mrs Roye (seated) is holding up a Coronation Mug. Gathered around her are Mrs Fielder, Mrs Lloyd, Mrs Thomas, Mrs Cooper, Mrs Stinton, Mrs Potts, Mrs Dickenson, Mrs Warrington, and Mrs Ashton.

The Tontine club, better known as the "Death and Dividend" Club, gathered for a coach tour in the 1930s, outside the Princess Hotel.

Westminister Road, Coronation Committee in 1953. On the left is Mrs Lee and on her left is Mrs E. Oliver. Mrs P. Catteral is fifth from the left and in the centre, wearing his Chain of Office, is the Chairman of the Council Mr P.H.Hall. On the extreme right is a future mayor, Mr F. Venables.

Six
The Village of Whitby

The town centre in 1907 was farm land belonging to Stud Farm. In 1814 many local cattle died of rinderpest and were buried under the site of the present Civic Hall. A caption to this postcard says, "A glimpse of new Whitby where sturdy oaks used to grow".

A horse and cart are coming down from the village of Whitby along a peaceful Whitby Road. The lane to the left is Arrowe Lane c.1908.

Behind the lamp post facing the thatched cottage can be seen Grange Farm. The Grange School which opened on the 6th January 1936, took its name from this farm, because it was built on part of its land.

The transport waggon in this photograph of main road, Whitby, is just passing the iron foundry of A.H. Norman, which sttod next to the White House at the corner of Arrowe Lane. Around some of the old streets you can still find manhole covers with "A.H. Norman" embossed on them.

This thatched cottage stood where the present Police Station stands. The last people to occupy it were members of the Percival family.

This is Arrowe Lane with Miss Gerrard's School on the right, behind school-yard railings. Further down the lane is the White House on the corner of Whitby Road.

This Church of England School in Arrowe Lane was built in 1891 for 80 infants. The average attendance is recorded as 69. The first teacher was Miss N.Gerrard. Later her sister Miss Mary E.Gerrard became the mistress.

The Church of St Thomas was built in 1909, and like the Catholic Church was made of corrugated sheets. When it was replaced by a new church, the old building was retained and used for many functions. Sadly it was burnt down in 1991.

This Methodist Chapel was built in 1873. It has now been demolished and replaced by a new one in Hope Farm Road. These trees have now gone and, set back from the road on the left, is the Youth Centre.

This is Whitby Road nearing the end of Chester Road as it enters the village. Here is "Bondy's Hill" and the allotments that faced the Sportman's Arms before the present shops were built.

Here are the shops mentioned above. In the distance can be seen the Water Tower that was built before the First World War to supply the village with water, replacing various wells and pumps.

The Parsonage Smithy was situated at the corner of Pooltown Road and Chester Road, alongside the Sportman's Arms. The business had its origins in 1873 when Harry Parsonage was sent by a Chester school to Mr J. Jones, a blacksmith with a smithy up the lane near to his house Bank Cottage, in Vale Road. Harry went as a bound apprentice to learn the blacksmith trade. In February 1879 he finished his apprenticeship and rented a house and the smithy from Mr Jones. By 1896 he had moved to this site and the smithy seen in the photograph.

The first of the houses on the left side is now the Driving Test Centre. The group of houses on the right were called Mount Pleasant (Michael Day Collection).

Where the shop is seen at the corner of Whitby Road and Vale Road stood the old village pump. The shop itself was built on the garden of an old farmhouse that belonged to a family called Meacock.

Sadly all these cottages in Vale Road have gone, but the family names live on in other parts of the Port. In the bungalow were the Jenkins, then came the Wrights, Tudors, Prices and Walkers.

These are the only two cottages to survivor. The left one is still called "Cash Cottage". The wooden hut was originally a sweet shop called Barrats, later to become a cobbler's shop.

This is Highbury House, the largest house in Vale Road in the 1930s. Standing outside (left) is Nurse Rendell with Mrs Kendall.

"Ivy Cottage", the oldest house in Vale Road. When being demolished a section was found to be made of wattle and daub and a date stone of 1671 was uncovered.

Just beyond the last house on the right was the start of "Bank Cottage" garden, containing its own well. A little further along was the lane that was built to give access to Jone's smithy.

The Old Fold was the name given to this group of cottages between the smithy lane and Whitby Old Hall on the corner of Stanney Lane. Most of the families living here worked for the Grace family.

These cottages in Stanney Lane stood at the entrance to Whitby Hall. They were constructed back to front, with the privies facing the hall, following an alleged dispute between the contractor and the Grace family at the hall.

These cottages in Stanney Lane were still drawing water from a pump in 1946 but soon after this taps were installed by the owner, Mr Wall.

Woodland Road was at one time a rough cart track with ditches and hedges that led to Stanney Wood, once the ancient fox covert owned by the Stanley family of Hooton Hall.

The first part of Woodland Road to be developed was opposite "Heath Farm" (where the "Woodlands" now is). Two cottages were built first, and then several houses. When all were occupied, three gas-street lights were installed to give the inhabitants a feeling of security.

The Cottage Hospital was originally built as a residence towards the end of the last century and called Heathfield House. It belonged to the Mansfield family.

During the First World War the house was purchased from them and converted into a hospital.

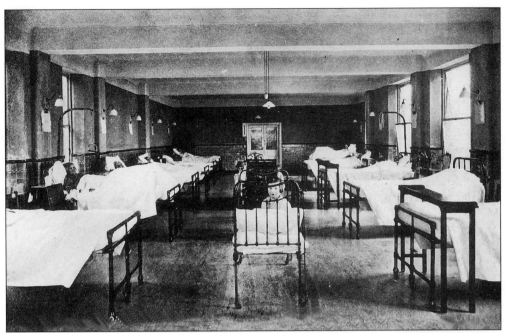

A children's ward at the hospital. An ambulance service provided by the British Red Cross was stationed at the hospital in 1925. A modern operating theatre was installed in the 1920s and a maternity and child welfare centre in 1929 (Michael Day Collection).

Nurse Annie Williams was one of the first midwives in Ellesemere Port. She started work in 1924 and served the community for 34 years. During this time she delivered over 3,500 babies.

"Garden City" was the local name given to these houses built at the turn of the century in Pooltown Road.

When first built they dominated the few remaining cottages. Their correct name is Pooltown Villas. The meadows are now occupied by a large housing estate.

Seven
Sports and Leisure

This view of the shoreline between Eastham and Ellesmere Port was taken in the early 1880s. A plan of 1802 shows that the canal terminal also had shooting butts and bath houses. An advert, in the Chester papers said, "The house at Ellesmere Port is neatly fitted up for the accommodation of those desirous of having lodging during the bathing season". There were baths for hot bathing in fresh and salt water and shower baths.

The Wirral Harriers outside the entrance to Hooton Hall. When the Stanley pack ceased hunting from Hooton Hall in 1868, the fox hounds were given up and a group of local gentlemen decided to hunt the hare on horseback and thus the Wirral Harriers were born.

For the first few seasons a pet deer was hunted. Hounds were never permitted to harm her and at the end of a run she was caught and conveyed to a paddock near Oxton Village. Sometimes she would run in a large circle eventually appearing at a gentle trot behind the pack.

Victoria Park was laid out by the S.U.R. Canal Co. for their employees to enjoy the peaceful setting in the early 1900s. It was landscaped and always kept neat and tidy.

In the good old summer time, band concerts were held in the park on Sundays. If the weather was nice the May Queen Festivities from Queen Methodist Church, seen in the background, were held here.

Whitby Hall, the former home of the Grace family, became Council Offices in 1931. In 1933 its surrounding 41 acres were laid out as a public park at a cost of £7,003.

Hooton Golf Club Ltd. was formed by a group of local businessmen on the 18th February 1924. This is the official opening of the new pavillion in 1927.

This is the Church Sunday School on its annual trip to New Brighton. The boat is the Eastham ferry boat Sapphire. The Church Band always accompanied the trip, and would play "Sweet Violets" on the way back.

This is the Ellesmere Port Public Silver Prize Band in 1900. Better known to everyone as the Chapel Band.

A trip on the Ship Canal for members and families of the Ellesmere Port Co-op Society. Just above the 'D' of the ship's name is a young boy standing with his sister. They are Christine and Raymond Agnew.

This is the same boat as above and the same trip in the 1930s. The boat is the W.E. Dorrington owned by the M.S.C.

In 1930 the Riveracre Valley was purchased from the Naylor Estate and in 1934 the Riveracre Baths was opened. It proved very popular with local people, and brought visitors from far afield as well.

A busy scene in the Riveracre Baths in the 1930s.

On the steps of the new Hippodrome in Carnegie Street in 1927 is the cast of *Our Miss Gibbs*. The men, from left to right: J. Halsall, W. Blain, T. Rigby, H.B. Worthington, J. Davis and W. Burke. The ladies, middle row: D. Athwood, V. Nall, M. Gell. Front row: M. Dallloway, M. Thomas and M. Willetts.

This is Danny Weir's chain gang, who appeared at many local fetes in the 1920s, dressed as convicts and winning many prizes.

The old Hippodrome was built between 1909 and 1910 in Meadow Lane. It was built as a variety theatre for Arthur Correlli and was later owned by Mr Bates of Stanney Grange Farm. From 1913 it operated as both a cinema and a theatre. Many locals appeared in shows here, either in theatrical groups or giving solo turns in talent shows. Because of a bad fire there in about 1908, the owner decided to build a new Hippodrome, next to the Majestic Ballroom in Carnegie Street, which he also owned.

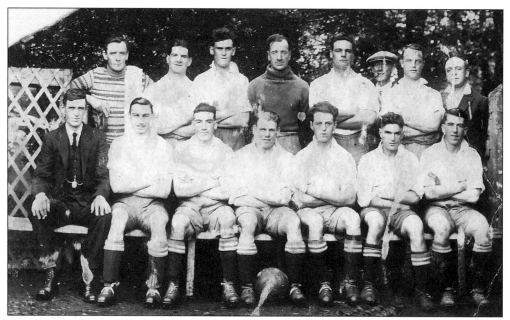

This is the Cement Works football team of 1929-30 season. They were admitted to the Cheshire County League in 1921-22, had four seasons in the league and retired in 1925.

Ellesmere Port's Victoria Football Club was established in the 1900s. This is the team for 1911-12.

Cambridge United football team in 1942. Front Row, left to right: Dorrington, Dorrington, J. Turner, J. Dykes, H. Reeves, Hope. Back row: J. Howard, E. Booth, T. Wilkie, G. Hickman, T. Winsor, Foulkes, H. Dorrington, M. Howard.

Ellesmere Port Football Club at a charity match during the Second World War. Front row, from left to right: Walters, Varney, S. Jenkins, T. Wilkie, T. Row. Back row, first three from the left: McNay, Mr Backhouse (the baker), C. Andrews, and on the extreme right, C. Price.

A group of Ellesmere Port Town A.F.C. supporters in glad array before departing for Crewe in their successful bid for the Cheshire Senior Cup on the 11th May 1957.

This is Stan Jenkins, the club secretary, holding up the cup which they won in 1957. They were also Cheshire League Champions for 1957/58, 1958/59, and 1959/60.

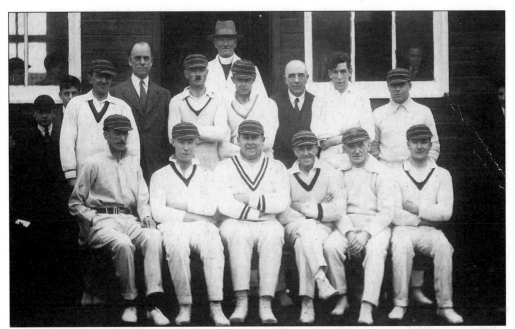

Ellesmere Port Cricket Team in the 1930s. Only two members have been identified, the captain Merrick Howard in centre at the front and H. Lathom, third from the right, back row.

McAlpine's Cricket Team in 1932. Front row, left to right: Foulkes, Hollingworths, H. Turner, M. Hughes, R. Rossin. Back row players: G. Turner, P. Lloyd, G. Jenkins, D. Hart, T. Wilkie and C. Hurd.

In the 1920s there was an athletic event called the "Great Walk" for boys under sixteen years of age. The route was from New Ferry to Ellesmere Port and back.

The competitors of the race shown here, included a youth from Ellesmere Port called Keeley who came from a famous sporting family in Whitby. The race was won by W. Kay.

Eight

Neighbouring Villages

Little Sutton, because of its position on the main road leading to the ferries, has always had more shops than most villages of its size. In the coaching manuals the Black Lion was a recognised place for a change of horses.

This is a view of Capenhurst Village from the West. On the right can be seen the ancient pinfold in which animals found straying on the highways were detained.

Christ Church, Capenhurst, was erected in 1859. Its unusual pagoda style steeple gets many admiring comments.

Cottages in Ledsham in the early years of the century. The village received a mention in the Domesday Book, although its name then was spelt Levetsham. The earliest present day spelling is recorded in 1387 as a mention in the Forest of Wirral Court, The Eyre.

Ledsham Station, seen here on the left, was from 1837 until 1863, the local railway station for Little Sutton and Ellesmere Port.

This is Beech Farm, Green Lane, Great Sutton. On the left of the picture can be seen the outline of the last village pump in Great Sutton. A bronze Age axehead was found here which is now kept in the Grosvenor Museum in Chester.

The White Swan, Great Sutton in the early 1900s. It had a number of stables at the rear to cater for the livery trade.

This is Chester Road, Little Sutton in about 1908. The shop where the white wall juts out near the centre of the picture is Walker's the chemist, at the corner of Walkers Lane.

This postcard of Little Sutton is dated April 1910. An X marked on the shop awning presumably marks the place where the writer lived or worked. This postcard sent to Somerset asked his friend if he would ever return.

Chester Road in Little Sutton. In the distance is an arcade over Coulter's shop. This wintry scene is believed to have been taken before the First World War.

Little Sutton's fire engine. The fire chief was Mr Cartwright, father of the present W. Cartwright, the builders. The fire engine was kept in a shed in their old yard, which was on the site of the present Presbyterian Church Hall.

The shop on the right is Lockett's Bakehouse and Corn Factors which stood on the corner of the Ledsham Road. This view is dated August 1904, and is one of the F. Walker series.

This is Coulter's shop in Little Sutton. In 1892 J.H. Coulter was a boot and shoe manufacturer at Liverpool House. Later the shop became a newsagent. The sign outside the shop says, Agent for Pullars Dye Works, Perth. Mrs Coulter is standing in the doorway.

The station was known as Sutton until 1886 when the name was changed to Little Sutton. This view of it was taken in 1909, before the footbridge was installed.

These are Midfield Terrace and Harrisons Terrace which link into Station Road. Rossmore Road West was built after the First World War by unemployed ex-servicemen. Harrisons Terrace was built in 1889, reputedly for workers in the Hooton & Little Sutton Gas Company, whose works were immediatly behind the houses.

The Wesleyan Church in Little Sutton as originally built in 1877.

THE VILLAGE. LITTLE SUTTON.
PERFECTION SERIES 1520.

The finger post on the left points the way to Ledsham Station and Birkenhead. On the right can be seen the Chemist Shop and Post Office, owned by F. Walker who made the series of Wirral postcards.

Law and Order. One of the two constables of the Cheschire Constabulary stationed at Little
Sutton Police Station was PC Ashton. This style of headgear was in use before the First World
War. Notice a constable with the same type of Headgear in the view of the Premier's visit to
Little Sutton in 1912 (opposite).

The scene outside the Old Red Lion before the arrival of the Prime Minister on July 20th 1912.

The Prime Minister Herbert Asquith can be seen standing in the open-back car in the centre of the picture on his visit to Little Sutton in 1912.

The people of Little Sutton are seen here celebrating the Coronation of King Edward VII in 1901. On the left is the Railway Hotel and in the centre is H. Bowyer's Pork Butchers who also had another shop, opposite the Knot, in Whitby Road.

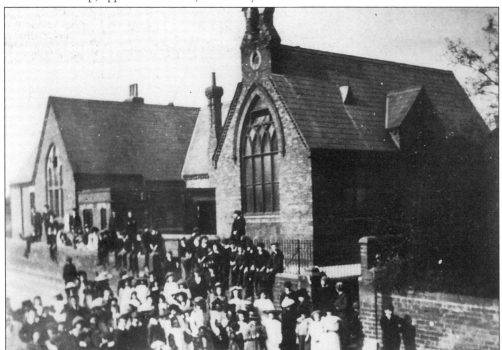

Berwick Road, Church School, was built in 1867. In the early days children paid to attend; 2d per week under 8 years and 3d per week if over. All the work was done with slates and pencils. On Chester Race Days no classes were held, so that children could watch the passing events and people.

This is old Sutton Hall. In 1798 Mr Joseph White of St James, Westminister, bought for £15,000 the manors or lordships of Great and Little Sutton, the 'Rectory' of Sutton, tithes in Little Sutton and Sutton Hall (then occupied by Ric. Amery). Underneath the chancel of Eastham Church are buried generations of the Whites of Sutton Hall. The last member of the family, Miss White of Chester, assigned on her death that the part of the church previouly owned by the Whites, to the Vicars of Eastham.

At one time there were two smithies in Little Sutton. One was called the top smithy and the other the bottom one. The top smithy was by the village well. Both businesses belonged to the Bennion Brothers, one was a wheelwright and the other a blacksmith.

The yew hedge is now all that remains in Ledsham Road of a medieval manor house belonging to the Abbot of St Werburg's Abbey, Chester. It was situated here for over three hundred years. In the field opposite, in 1811, farmworkers clearing it for re-use, discovered under the surface a graveyard for the monks.

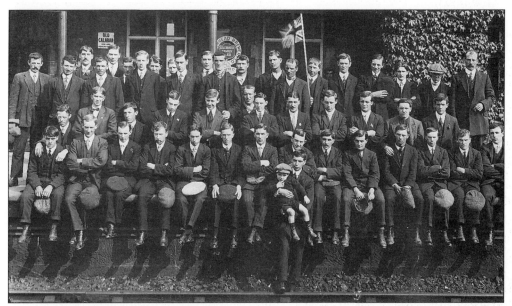

Little Sutton Station in 1914. A group of local men were photographed before going off to war. The man with the little boy is Sam Worral and the little boy is Walter Cartwright. There are seven brothers of the Lloyd family in the picture; Sam, Bob, George, Tom, David, and Stephen of Hooton Green. Only one, Stephen, was killed in action, and his name is on the Cenotaph in Childer Thornton.

King George V inspects a guard of honour of the Boy's Brigade at Hooton Station in 1914.

Police Station and Reading Room, Little Sutton.

The staff of Little Sutton Police Station consisted of a sergeant and two constables. The Station Sergeant can be seen in the photograph standing to the left of the tree.

This scene looks back from the Police Station, across the road to the Railway Hotel and the Old Red Lion.

Here is PC Ashton again, this time with a traditional helmet and a bicycle photographed in the 1920s. On his sleeve he has a St John's Cross Badge awarded for First Aid.

On the road to Hooton Station in the early 1900s.

Hooton Station.

Hooton Station in 1908. The chimmney stack in the background is part of Hooton Brickworks, the largest in the area, and at the time employing 49 men.

The church of St Paul was built between 1858 and 1862 by R.C. Naylor who owned Hooton Hall at this time. An unusual feature is the cloister walk that connects the church with a private family entrance. The architect was J. Colling and cost of building was £5,000.

These one-roomed lodges on either side of the main gates were used as a house. One side was a bedroom, and the other a combined kitchen and dining-room.

These two photographs were taken by the local photographer F. Walker. Both show groups of local people gathered outside St Pauls Parish Church, Hooton, for an open air service to celebrate the Coronation of King George V and Queen Mary on the 22nd June 1911.

The old hunting bridge over the Riveracre Road. The road started at the Chester Road Gate and went over this bridge to Hooton Hall. After passengers had alighted from their carriages, they were driven away to the stables through a pond to clean the carriage wheels.

This view of Hooton Hall is not often seen and was taken from the racecourse which was situated at the back of the main buildings.

This old view of Childer THornton shows on the left School Lane, called after the old school that stands further up on the right. The village has a number of houses of great age and character.

This old house has a date stone of 1746 above the door. The address written on the front shows the writer was stationed at nearby Hooton Hall during the First World War.

A charming scene at West View, Childer Thornton in the early 1900s.

Thornton Hall was once the home of one of the Jones family, a director in the family-owned Wolverhampton Corrugated Ironworks. For a number of years now it has been a hotel, changing its name with each new owner.

Childer Thornton Carnival in 1950 was held in Bob Davies' field. Here we see the Page of Honour making a declaration before the Coronation of the Carnival Queen.

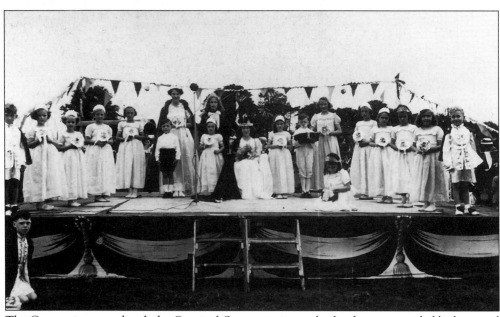

The Coronation completed, the Carnival Queen sits in regal splendour surrounded by her royal retinue.

Childer Thornton Coronation festivities in 1953. Both School Lane and New Road are decked out in flags and buntings and the children are in their fancy dress. Is the main character here an early version of 'The Lady likes Milktray'?

Acknowledgements

This book has only been made possible by the generosity of many kind people who have lent treasured family pictures and shared their memories to show, once and for all, that this town is one to be proud of, one with its own history and character. So thanks to all who made it possible:

Mr G. Ankers, Mr J. Ashton, Mr Bearcroft, Mrs Boughie, Mrs P. Catteral and her sister, Mr R. Craven, Mrs Day (née Keeley), Mr L. Doylerush, Mrs B. Fletcher, Mrs P. Green, Mr R. Hignett, Mr T. Lardner, Mrs T. Lee, Mr H. Percival, Mr C. Pitcher, Mrs B. Saban, Mrs B. Simpson, Mr L. Smith, Mr T. Wilkie, Mr T. Williams, Mr H.B. Worthington.

I am also grateful for the help given by the following:

The Boat Museum Trust, Mr G. Fisher, Ellesmere Port Chief Librarian and the Reference Library staff. Mr M. Day for restoration work on old photographs, Mr J.M. Capp of Australia, for all the material on H.M. Ordnance Factory, and last but not least Mary, Carol and staff at Max Spielman's for their help.

I dedicate this book to my wife Norah Rowena and the people of Ellesmere Port.